Jinia M

Quotes

1

A Lift In Life
The Unsatisfied Soul

also by
Jinia M

Jinia M
Quotes

Book of 100 life quotes.

Fill yourself.....

Dedicating this book to everyone my family,
friends and near ones.

I AM ONLY AN EMPLOYEE OF THAT
EMPLOYER WHO RUNS THE
UNIVERSE!

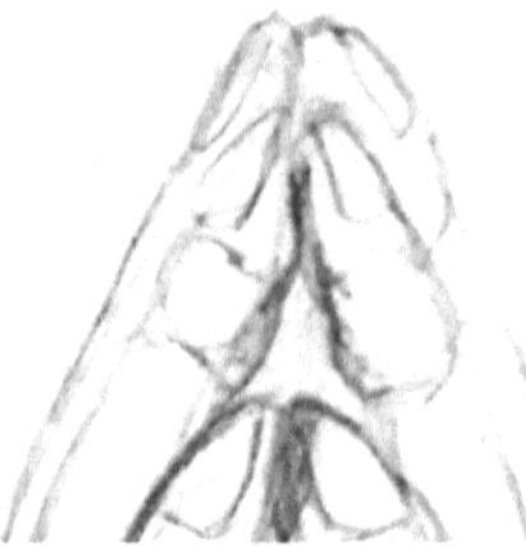

I just want the world to remember me as one of God's favourite daughters.

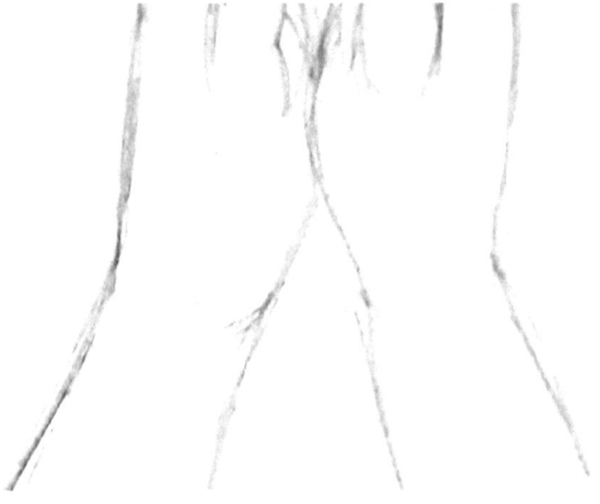

You are allowed to change the future.

The fact is you are never out of love.
Never out of your love.

You were still breathing before
him
/her.

Once you visited your home inside yourself you will never try to find a home in others!

Quitting never gives you happiness!

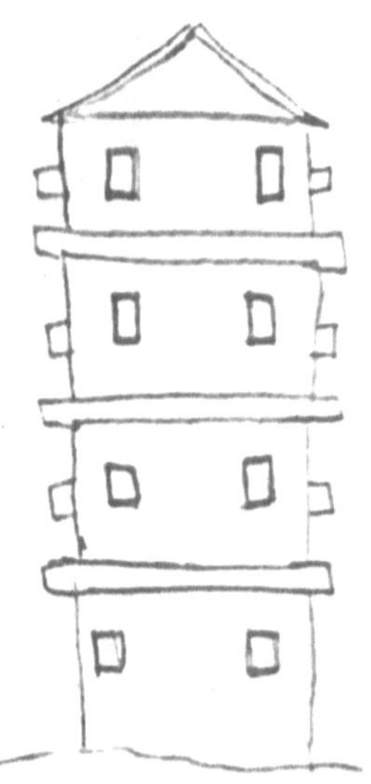

Build your empire, where peace lasts.

Today indulge some moments in

self-care.

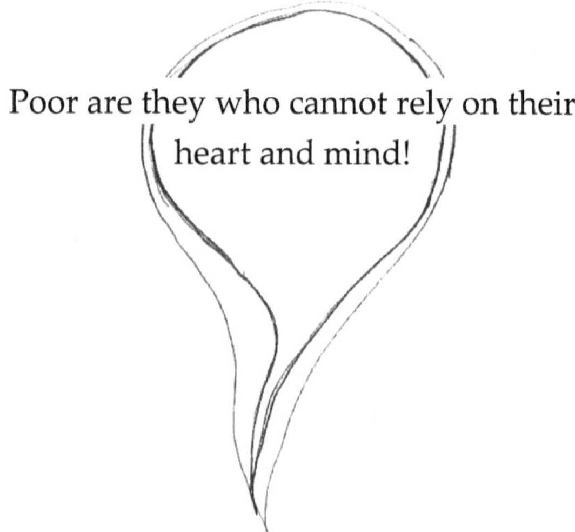
Poor are they who cannot rely on their
heart and mind!

Invest your time in something
that explains you.

You will survive.

Your scar is beautiful that shows how
strong you are!

When you see the doors are closing then focus on the door that is about to open.

Your future awaits!

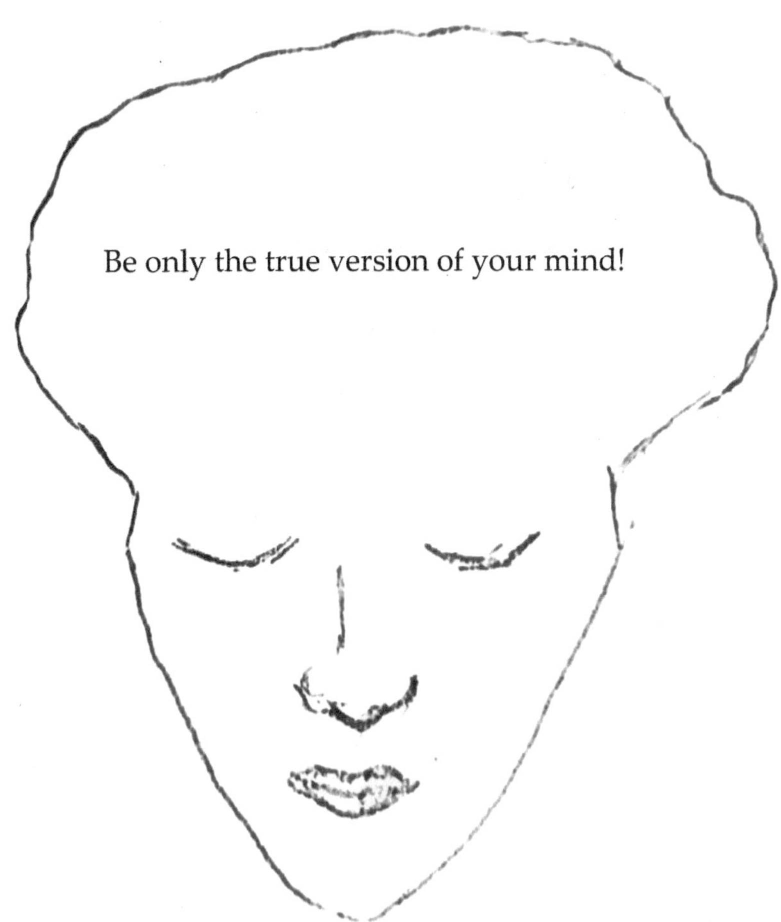

Be only the true version of your mind!

CHOOSE FAITH OVER FEAR!

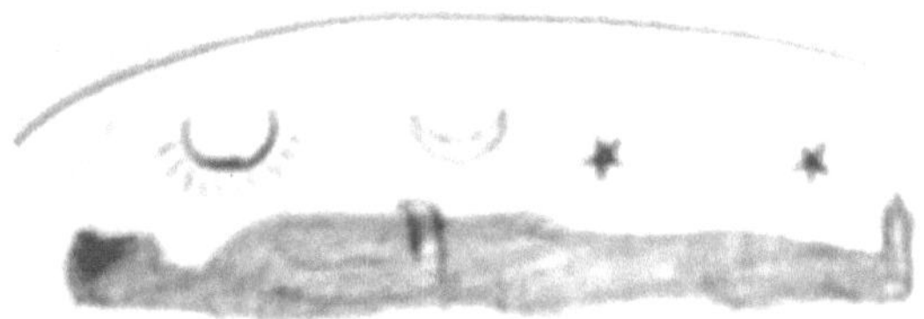

Sometimes when you can't see the next move, relax for your universe is in the creation of it and will reveal it to you at the correct timing!

Self-love is not for some moment.

It is a journey of every moment.

Learning every moment.

Indulging in every moment.

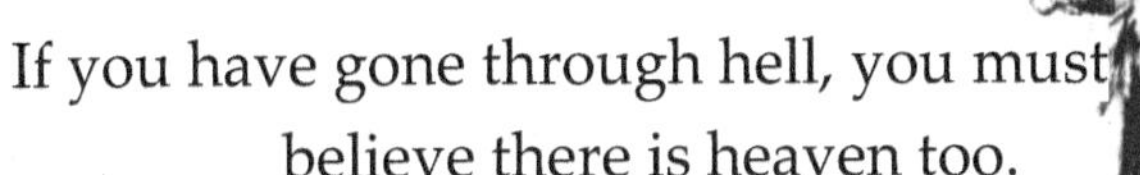

If you have gone through hell, you must
believe there is heaven too.

Your belief will become your coming
future and beyond!

"It takes a journey to become the person of your heart. You cannot wake up one morning and say I am formed".

You have to go through the ups and downs of life given challenges and one day you will reach where you belong.

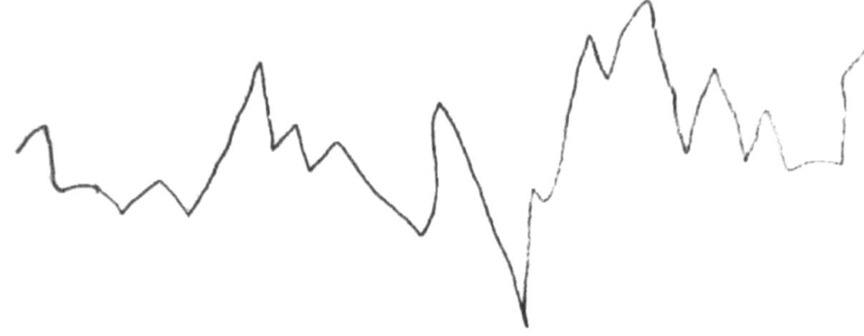

Time never stops for anyone so you should never stop for anyone!

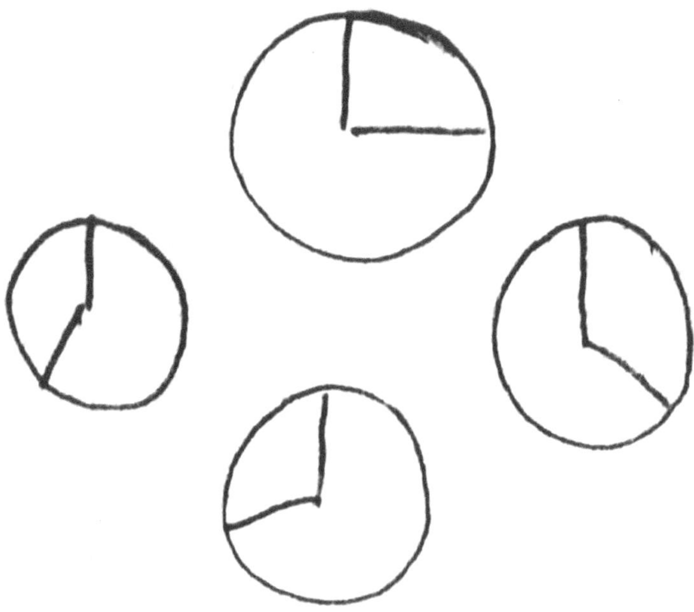

Never stop believing in your dream!

You have enough power to create your
own world. Why wait??

A soul is always free.
Be a free soul.

How you use your time is life!

Relax you are not the one who is
responsible for everything happening
around you.
Be gentle with your heart.

A fall is indicating your next rise.
Only when you believe!

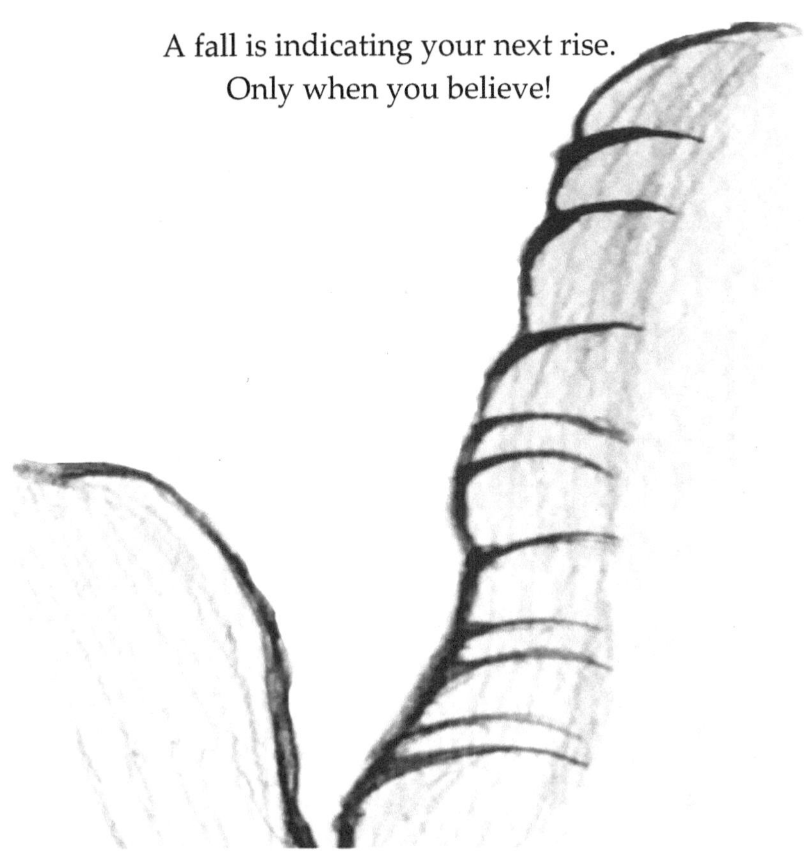

"
Give yourself 20 minutes every day.

Detached yourself from the world at that time. Keep looking in the sky or any part of nature. Bring yourself out. You will slowly learn your presence.

"

If you do not believe in miracles, you
can never see any miracle.
True that!

Doubting yourself is a sign of fear!

Lifelike tides always go ups and down
to shape the beauty of the gift, that we
have received!

If you want to be strong from your heart
then hold the honesty with all your
heart.

Live a truthful life.
The universe will always stay close to
you!

If you can't find peace within yourself.
You are never going to find peace in
anyone!

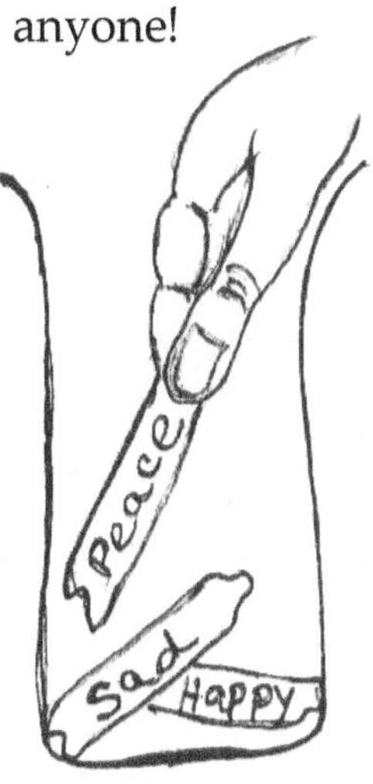

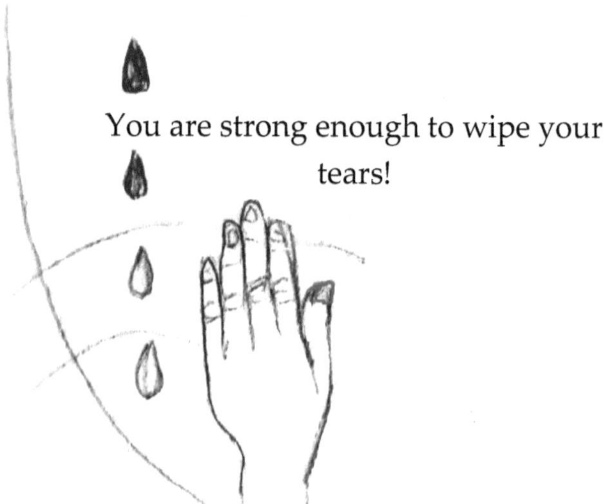

You are strong enough to wipe your tears!

I never say don't cry.
Cry as much as you want.
But when you finished crying wipe your
tears yourself!

And move to the next step of your life.

If you have never cried.

You will never understand smile!

43

Earn respect and love will follow.

There is no one on this earth to replace you.

So be you.

Sometimes your focus needs more focus
to progress.

Give your time some time to bloom.

When you know that something is not meant for you then you have all the right to control your attraction towards it.

No matter how much you learn
yourself, a part of you will always
remain unknown to you.

Our words tell others who we are.

Our work tells others what we are.

If you have to control everything around you in your life then you will remain the most unhappy person in this one life.

When you see life is not moving forward, you should know that your heart and mind are residing in the past only.

Don't ask for help

try to make it a habit to be your help.

We are climbing 365 steps every year.

every day

every night

in task

in halt

in giggles

in grief

in fall

in rising.

If you want to know how life is at the age of twenty, you have to travel all the nineteen years.

If you want to know how life is at thirty, you have to travel twenty-nine years.

The math is as simple as that.

Life is sometimes only to break the
monotonousness!

You don't know what store on the other
side of the bank keeps rowing your boat
– keep moving with hope.

You are not broken you have got the
opportunity to recreate yourself!

When you are recreating yourself just remember that it should be designed by the deepest desire that you have for yourself!

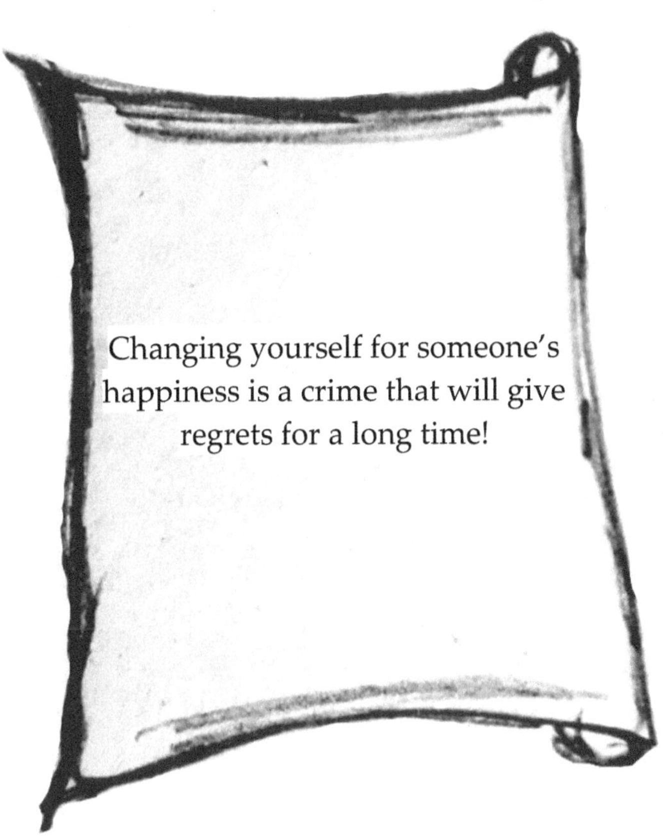

Changing yourself for someone's
happiness is a crime that will give
regrets for a long time!

Patience is growth and
growth is inevitable

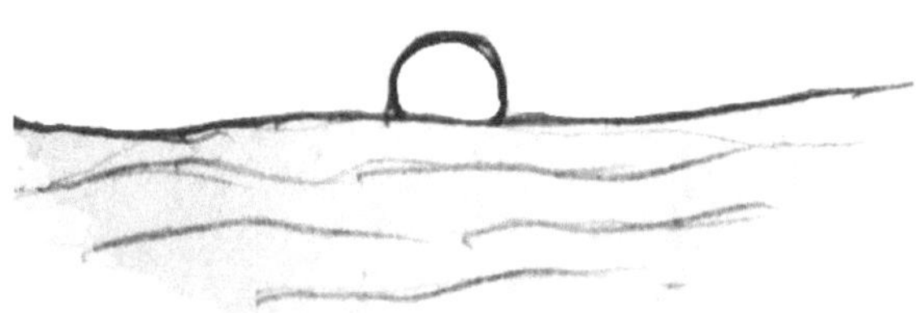

You know who you are. So do not waste your time listening to the people who never try to step inside your heart. Get up and get going you have an ocean to cross!

Build yourself, build your home, build
your world. You have the power to
create to leave your mark for the good.

There is always a world inside.

You have to wait.

Maybe you are working very hard but you have to wait for the result.

You cannot ask the result to come to you at your time. Be cautioned.

Your journey is to work and destiny is earned!

Everything is possible when you believe
in two words

'I Can'!

Happiness doesn't depend on anyone's absence or presence!

Give love
Give respect
To yourself first.
Be kind
Be humble
With yourself first.

Truth is like light
either you keep it on for
your endurance
or keep it off for
darkness.

Your prayers will be answered!

A day will come soon when the sun will tell you that the pain is over. You are now free to smile.

What exactly we are doing while
moving forward....

We are leaving our footsteps behind so
that someone can follow!

"I know that I am lying on this floor in more than a thousand pieces, but I also know that I won't be here like this forever".

There is a difference between accepting the present situation and believing in the **rise.**

(Choose)

One day you will thank yourself for
trying!

If you can't then no one can and if you
can then no barrier can stop you!

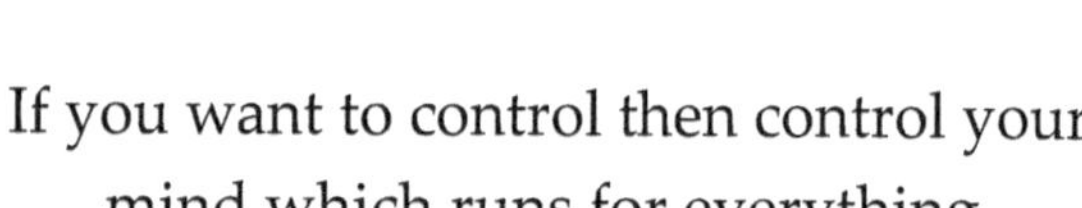

If you want to control then control your
mind which runs for everything.

When your mind tells you to work,
work.
When your body tells you to rest, *rest.*
As simple as that.
Don't try to run for things ignoring
yourself!

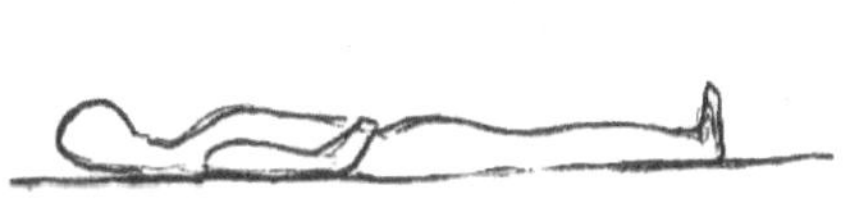

I understand life isn't beautiful, but believe me you have everything you need inside you to make this life beautiful.

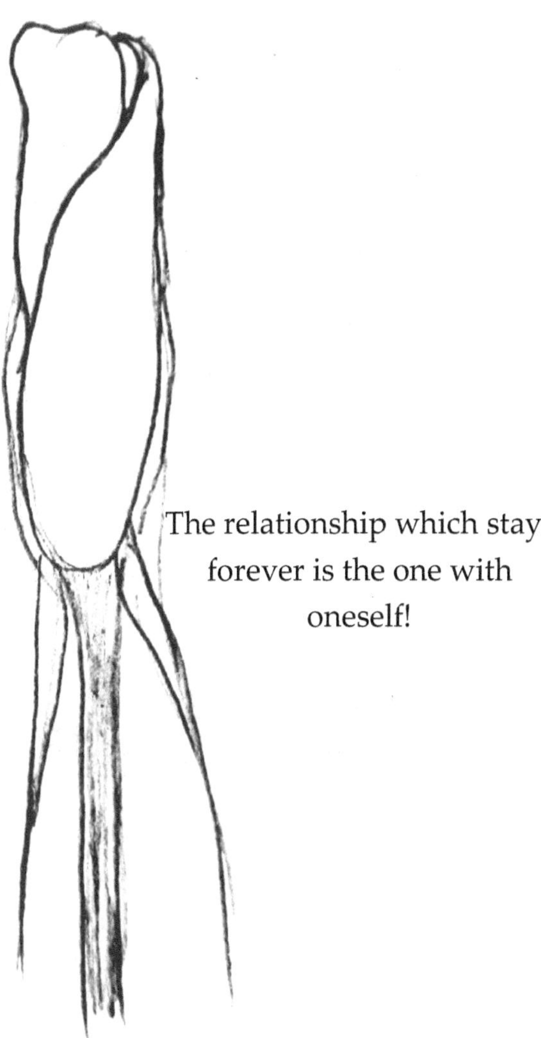

The relationship which stays
forever is the one with
oneself!

What a fool you are.
When someone rejects you
You reject yourself.
Telling yourself worthless.

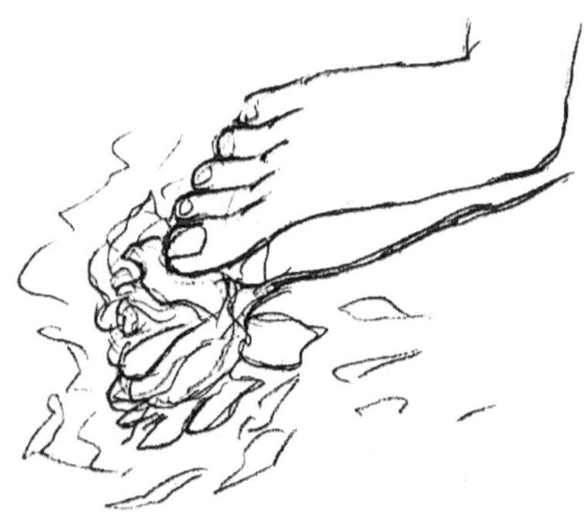

A calm mind is the absence of fear!

Many times, we get lost just to be found
in a new way!
Do not let yourself down in this period.
This phase is also important!

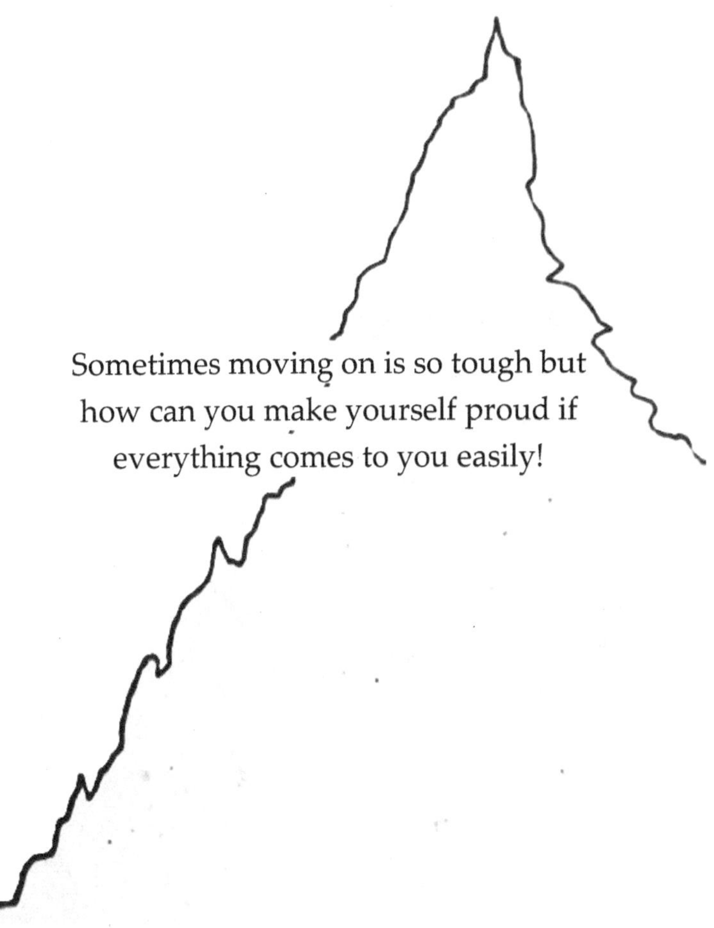

Sometimes moving on is so tough but how can you make yourself proud if everything comes to you easily!

It's not possible to be with the right people all the time, so be your company.

If you cannot become someone's smile, at least do not become the reason for their tears!

Believe in progressing in life.
Not only thinking and looking back.

You need hard work to become a rich
person. But you do not need any hard
work to be a human.
It's simple.

$$\{2 + 2 = 4\}$$

Your weakness blames others.

Fall in love with the word 'possible'.

Success is not about showing the world
who you are.
Success is about knowing and learning
who you are!

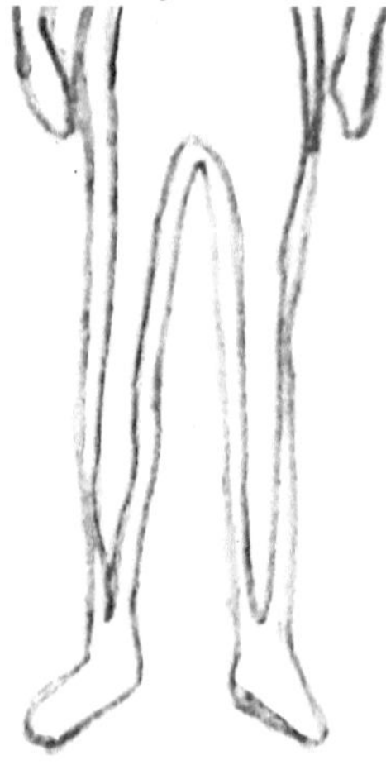

Your dreams are your hidden wings.

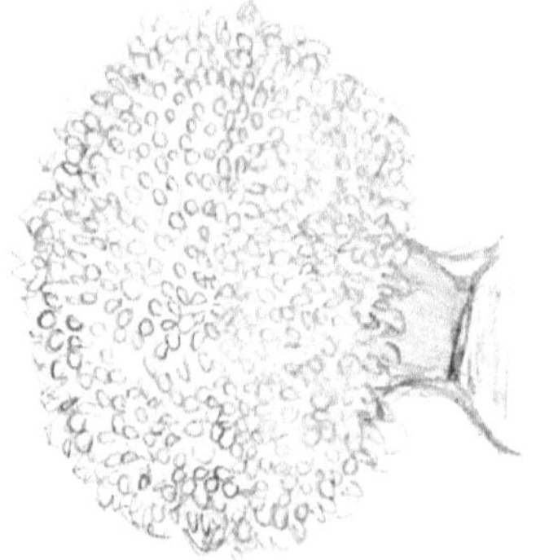

Your work is your power.
Invest your mind in your work.

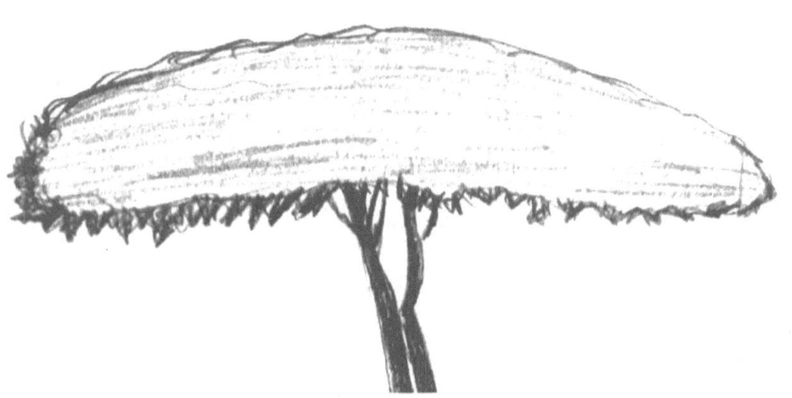

Do not ask for shelter.
Be your shelter.

Time takes time to form!

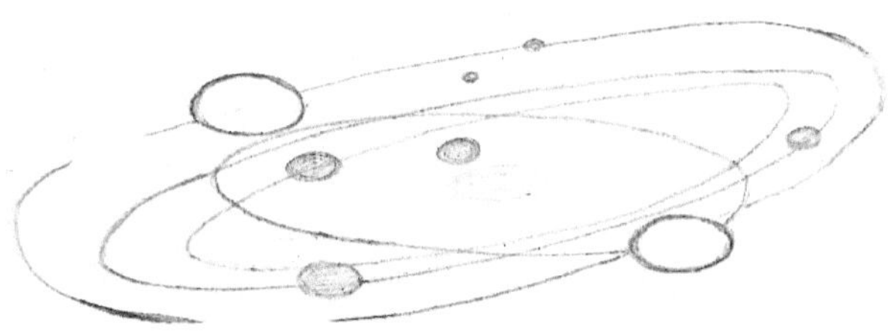

With that faith in your heart.
You have stepped into the beautiful
corner of your mind.
Now go and spread yourself,
you are all set to fly!

One moment you are down and the other moment you will be up. Take care of all your downs and eventually, you will enjoy your ups.

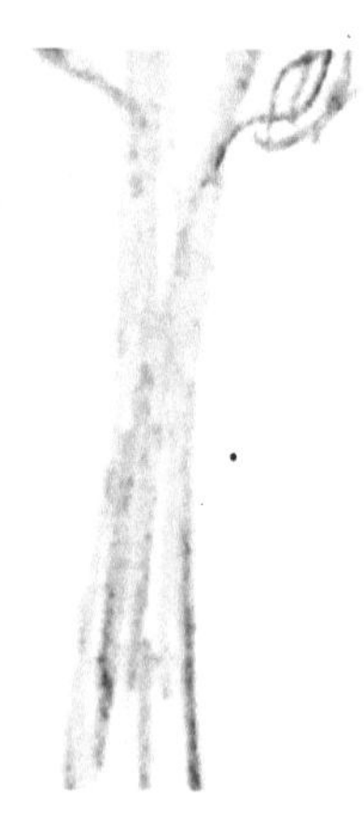

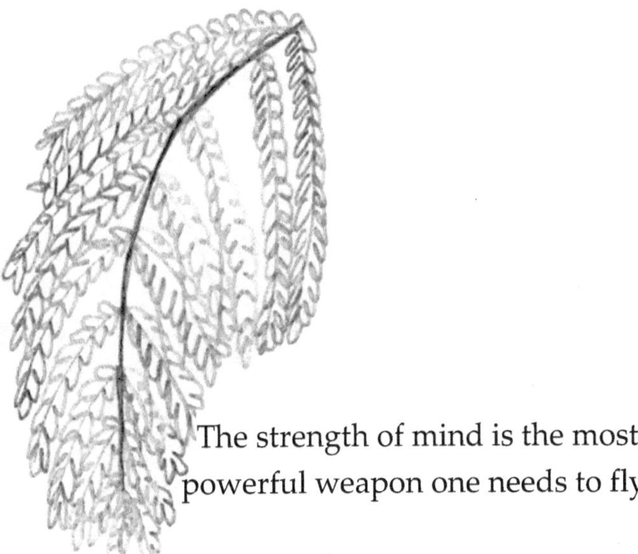

The strength of mind is the most powerful weapon one needs to fly!

Once a weak part is broken it won't
remain weak!

Blind
Deaf
Dumb
Orphan
Aged
Foodless
Homeless
Handicapped
Which one are you????

(Before you give up…)

Even these people fight with challenges.

Food you need,
home you need,
clothes you need,
work you need.
But what you don't need is weakness
and fear to be alone!

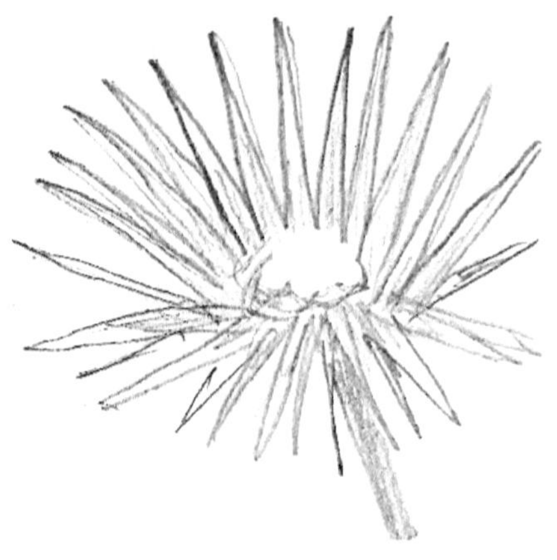

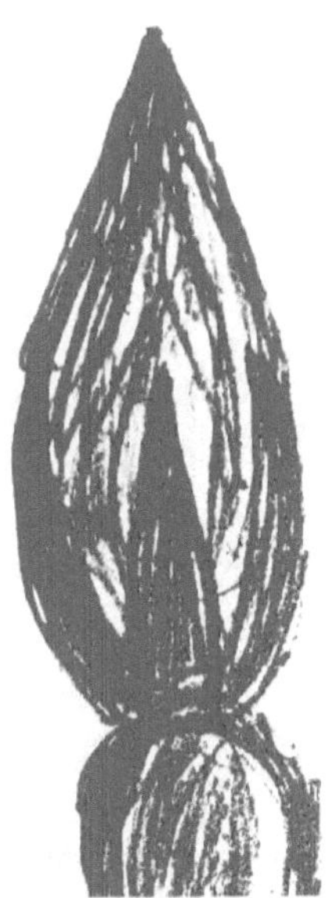

Choose loneliness over negative company!

Be a student throughout your life!

The solutions are often hidden in the
problems.
What we need is to focus!

Your dreams are your secrets.
Don't share your secrets!

Remember every day is a learning day!

What is the strongest among the human
body part?
It is the heart which dies countless
deaths and born again from the
residues!

It's only you who will understand your heart and say exactly what it tells you to say. It's only the dreams of your mind which only should control your action and your words. It's only the rhythm of your heartbeats that you must understand and allow them to control your arms and body. *It should be you and you.* Your true self is the one which live with you, the one who stays with you, the one who is crying with you, laughing with you, struggling with you, learning and growing with you, enjoying with you. The one that is inside your body. Your thoughts speak to you when you are kind to yourself, care for yourself, and live for yourself. Being you is not a limited-time work but loving and being you is your lifetime...

Author's words

"A book is not written to have readers. A book is born through the connection of a soul with the universe. A book is not just pages with words it has a presence like souls born on earth. A book can be written with experiences but experience has to be a change in that soul. A book is a mere presence to many people but a book's presence can become change many hearts, thoughts and decisions. A book is not just a work of an author or publisher, a book is that light that can pass through you to make you feel you. A book can become anyone's companion because its silent presence is enough to speak the heart. Books are only the medium through which people can reach their inner depth.

Fall in love with reading and feel the presence of souls on this earth. Maybe you can be surprised by the changes that occur in your thoughts. Maybe you will feel or see life the way it has never opened up to you. Maybe you are chosen one to feel different like never before or like the distinctive way.

A book is a one-time buy but a presence of a lifetime. A true friend forever."

About the author

A poetess, a novel writer, and a painter herself put all her thoughts and skills into writing books. Her first published book 'A Lift In Life' came out as a lift to her own life. She never thought of becoming an Author ever. But it has flown out from her heart as if everything was pre-decorated and embedded in her soul. In the year 2015, she met with an accident that destroyed her physical strength but she rose only by practising yoga for one and a half years. She wanted to start a career as a content writer. But her subconscious mind landed her to be an author. She was naive with her mind when she thought of writing something to share with the world. But her self-love and self-compassion were the only strength to embark on the journey. She wrote her first book in 2019, but she started her self-publishing by reprinting her first and second books in 2021.

Born and brought up in Kolkata (city of joy), India. She doesn't represent her country, culture or religion. She is only a soul when it comes to writing and painting thus; writes her name as Jinia M. Her full name is Jinia Mondal.

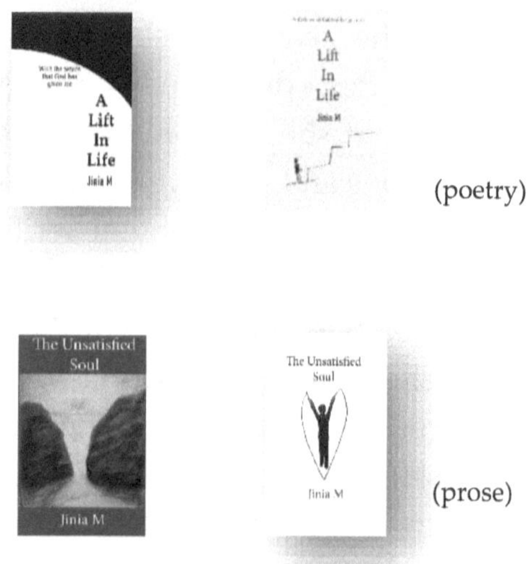

(poetry)

(prose)

Shop at the website
www.jiniamondal.com/shop

<u>Follow social accounts</u>.

Instagram @ **wordsinpen**
Facebook @ **wordsinpen**
Twitter @ **Jinia_Mondal**
Email: jinia.thoughts@gmail.com.

{Keep following the social accounts for daily inspiration and to know the upcoming works.}

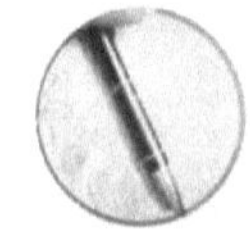

Jinia Mondal publishing